jim brickman
love songs & lullabies

piano / vocal / chords

project manager:
jeannette de lisa

book art layout&design:
**michael caprio,
caprio media design (l.a.)**

photography:
david rose

love songs & lullabies

prelude

little stars

love never fails

shades of white

above the clouds

night prayer

i see the moon

dreamland

safe and sound

beautiful (as you)

course of love

you

love songs & lullabies

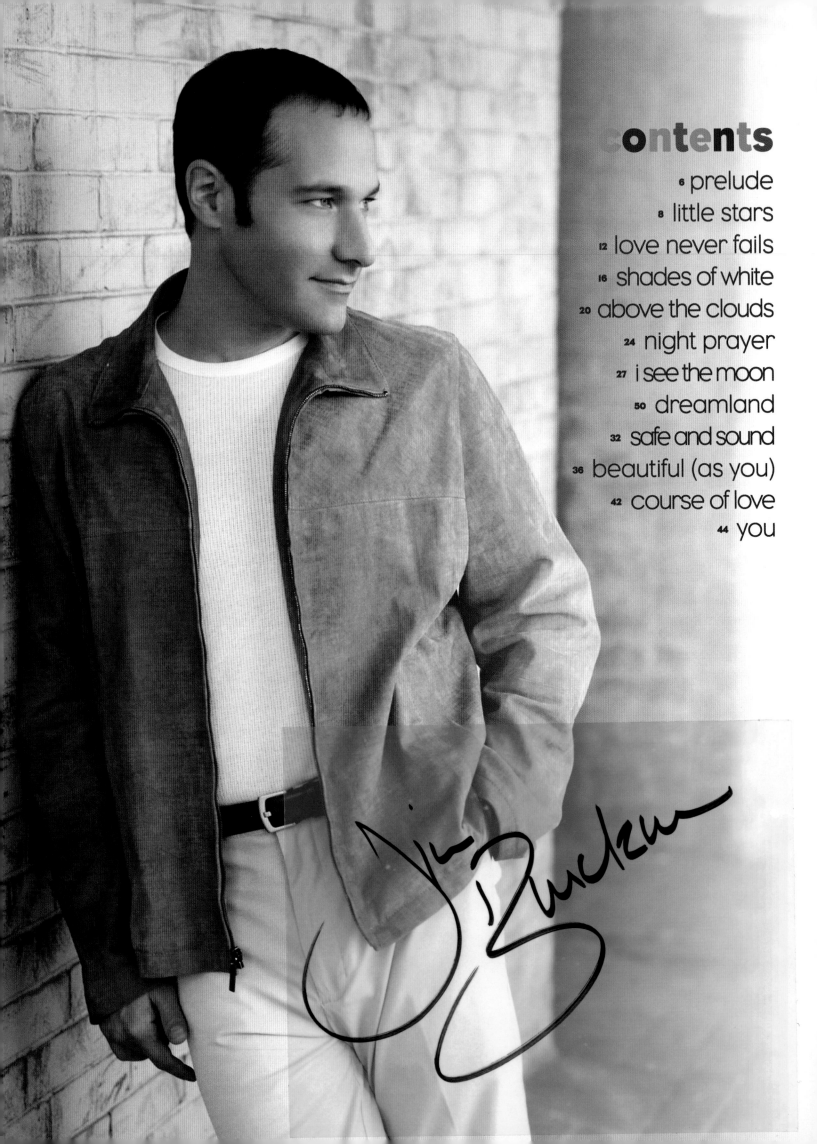

contents

6 prelude

8 little stars

12 love never fails

16 shades of white

20 above the clouds

24 night prayer

27 i see the moon

50 dreamland

32 safe and sound

36 beautiful (as you)

42 course of love

44 you

the romantic sounds of **jim brickman**

the complete jim brickman catalog

valentine

This IMPORT ONLY compilation features some of Jim's favorite hits including "Valentine," "The Gift," "Simple Things," and "Love of My Life." CD also features some of Jim's most-loved piano instrumentals.

simple things

This CD features classic Brickman solo piano recordings as well as the hit song "Simple Things" with Rebecca Lynn Howard, "It Must Be You" with All-4-One, and "A Mother's Day."

my romance

Jim's live CD featuring guest stars Donny Osmond, Olivia Newton-John, David Benoit, and Dave Koz. Includes the hits "Valentine," "Love of My Life," "Partners in Crime," and more.

destiny

Features the hit "Love of My Life" with Michael W. Smith, the title song, and guest performances by Carly Simon, Pam Tillis, Herb Alpert, Jordan Hill, Billy Porter, and more.

ballads

LIMITED EDITION INTERNATIONAL IMPORT featuring the best of Jim Brickman. Available only through Brickman Music. NOT AVAILABLE in any stores in North America.

visions of love

A collection of love songs by vocalists including Anne Cochran and her hit "After All These Years" as well as performances by Janis Ian and Phil Perry. Also features Dave Koz.

the gift

Jim's holiday album featuring the #1 hit title song with Collin Raye and Susan Ashton as well as guest performances by Kenny Loggins and Point of Grace. A holiday favorite!

picture this

Features Jim's #1 hit "Valentine" with Martina McBride as well as the instrumental favorites "Dream Come True," "Picture This," "First Steps," "Edgewater," and more.

by heart

Jim's second CD, which features the hit title song as well as the instrumental hit "Angel Eyes." Also includes "Lake Erie Rainfall," "If You Believe," "In a Lover's Eyes," and more.

no words

Appropriately titled, this CD is Jim's first recording, which features beautiful piano solos such as "Rocket to the Moon," "Heartland," "Still," "So Long," "Shaker Lakes," and more.

other items...

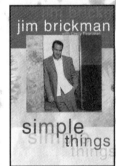

simple things

Simple Things is a collection of humorous, poignant essays that will help you get out of the fast lane and savor life's true pleasures—from a vacation in your own neighborhood to holding a newborn baby for the first time. In his soothing yet pointed manner, Brickman mulls over how to get back to basics when it comes to life's big topics—such as love, health, finances, romance, parenting, and friendships. *Simple Things* is about opening your eyes: To life. To love. To friendship. And to ordinary miracles that make each day so sweet.

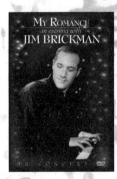

my romance

Available on both DVD and VHS, this live concert of Jim's PBS special features guest stars Donny Osmond, Olivia Newton-John, Dave Koz, Anne Cochran, and Tracy Scott Silverman. Includes footage not originally seen on the national TV broadcast.

love songs & lullabies

the cd:

Jim's first lullaby record features a collection of original lullabies as well as Jim's interpretations of some classics. The CD also features the love songs "Love Never Fails" with Amy Sky, "Course of Love" from the CBS daytime drama "Guiding Light," and two songs from his PBS special of the same name, "You" with Ally McBeal's Jane Krakowski and "Beautiful (As You)" with All-4-One.

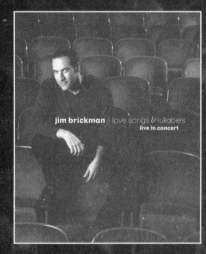

the vhs/dvd:

Jim's second PBS special features footage not seen on the original broadcast as well as performances by guest stars Jane Krakowski (from TV's "Ally McBeal"), Kevin Spirtas (from "Days of Our Lives"), pop group All-4-One, Beth Nielsen Chapman, Anne Cochran, Joshua Payne, and Tracy Silverman. Highlights include stirring piano solos, a "Patriotic Medley," a "Sesame Street" tribute, and more.

PRELUDE

By JIM BRICKMAN

Moderately slow, with expression

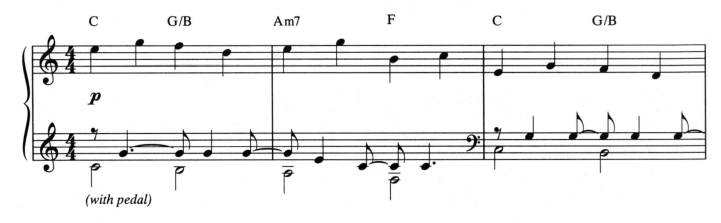

(with pedal)

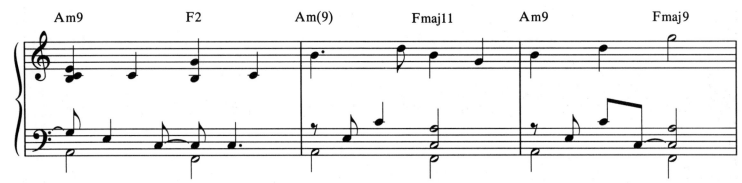

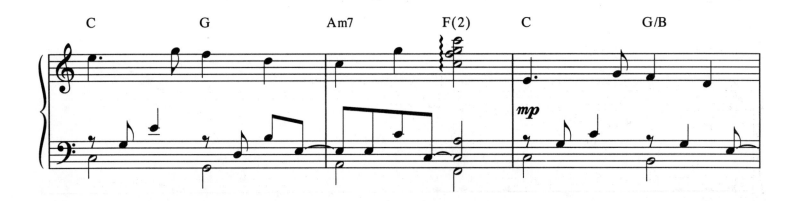

poco rit.

accel.

With more motion

LITTLE STARS

By JIM BRICKMAN

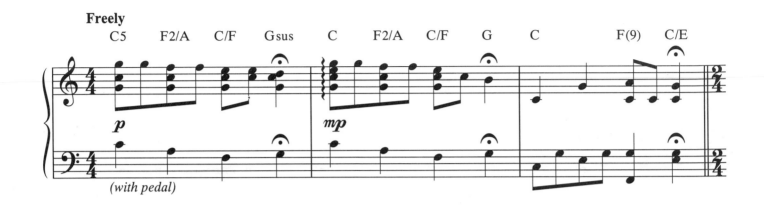

LOVE NEVER FAILS

Music by J.S. BACH
Text: I Corinthians 13
Arranged and Adapted by
AMY SKY and MARC JORDAN

Slowly ♩ = 72

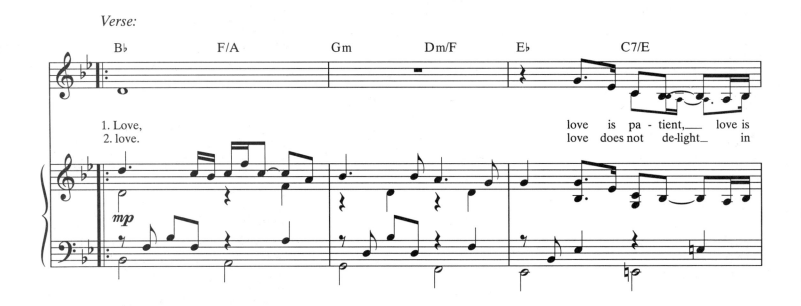

Verse:

14

give to you___ faith, hope and

hope and love.___

Chorus:

Love nev-er fails,___ nev-er fails. I prom-ise you, my___

SHADES OF WHITE

By JIM BRICKMAN

ABOVE THE CLOUDS

By JIM BRICKMAN

Moderately ♩ = 80

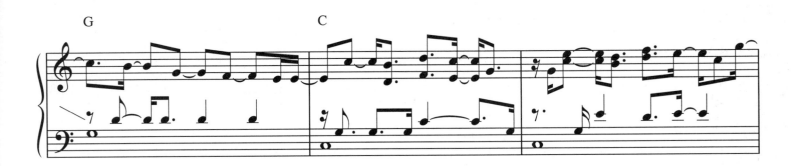

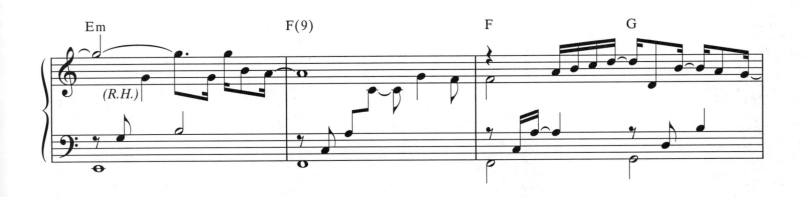

Above the Clouds - 4 - 1
PFM0214

NIGHT PRAYER

By JIM BRICKMAN

I SEE THE MOON

By JIM BRICKMAN

SAFE AND SOUND

By JIM BRICKMAN

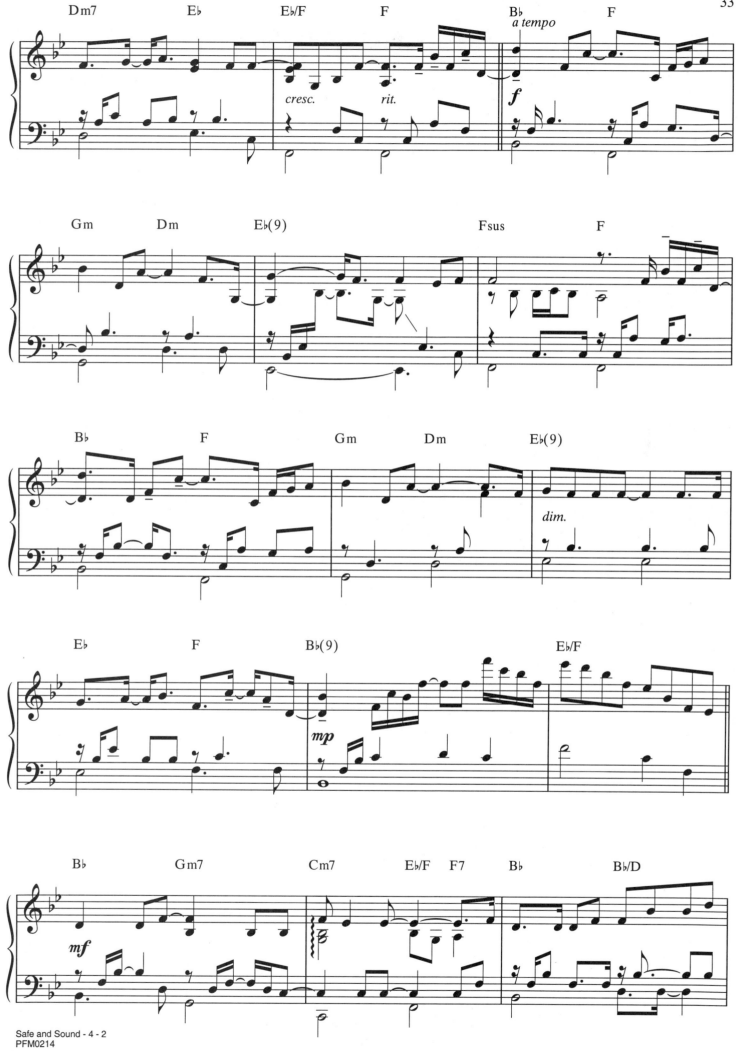

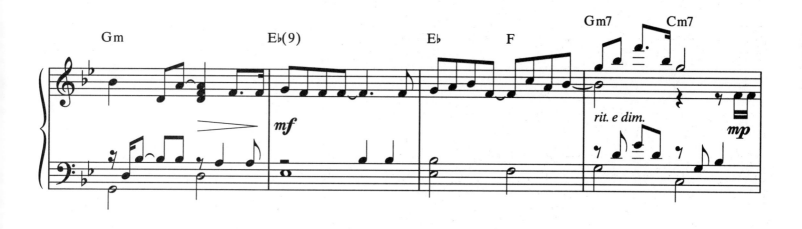

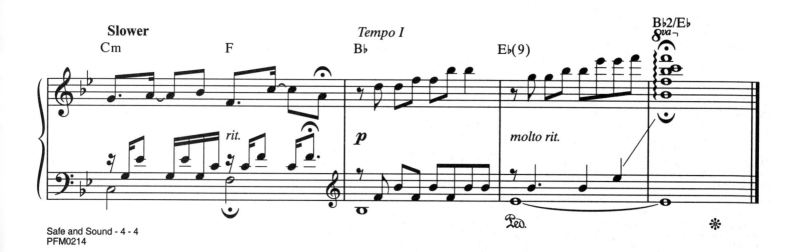

BEAUTIFUL
(AS YOU)

Words and Music by
JIM BRICKMAN, JACK DAVID KUGELL
and JAMIE JONES

Slowly and freely ♩ = 60

Verse:

1. From the mo-ment I saw____ you, from the mo-ment I looked___ in-to___ your eyes,___
2. *See additional lyrics*

And when it comes to shoot-ing stars,__ I have seen__ a few._____ But I've

nev - er seen__ an - y - thing_____ as beau - ti - ful.___ No, I've

nev - er seen__ an - y - thing_____

as beau - ti - ful___ as___ you.

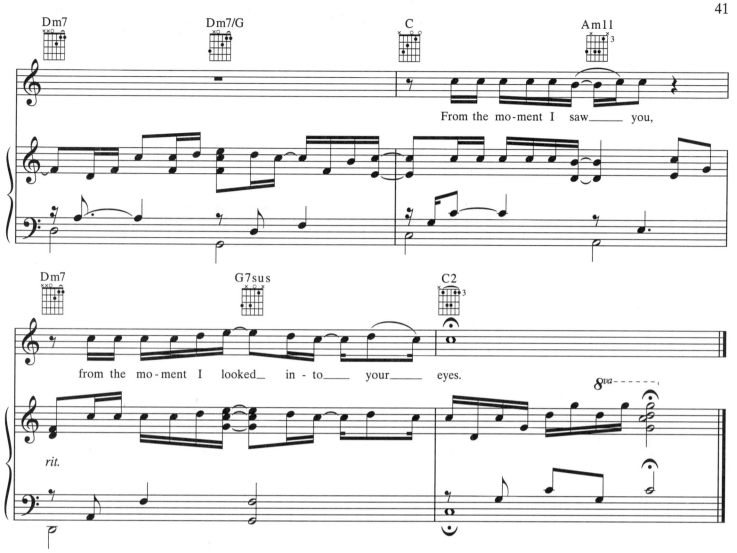

Verse 2:
I can't believe that I have you,
I can't believe that you're here in my arms.
I've been waiting a lifetime for you, for you.
And I've dreamed about you,
Pictured in my mind what I would see.
But I never imagined just how beautiful you'd be.
(To Chorus:)

COURSE OF LOVE

By JIM BRICKMAN
and BRIAN SIEWERT

YOU

By JIM BRICKMAN,
DANE DE VILLER and SEAN SYED HOSEIN

Verse:

1. I nev-er felt__ a-lone,__ I was hap-py on__ my own.__
2. I nev-er thought that love__ would be__ such a cu-ri-os-i-ty.__

And who would ev-er know__ there was some-thing miss-ing?
What at-tract-ed you__ to me__ was so un-ex-pect-ed.

do_____ with-out you.__

Whoa,_____

D.S. ℅ al Coda

48

You - 6 - 5
PFM0214

DREAMLAND

By JIM BRICKMAN

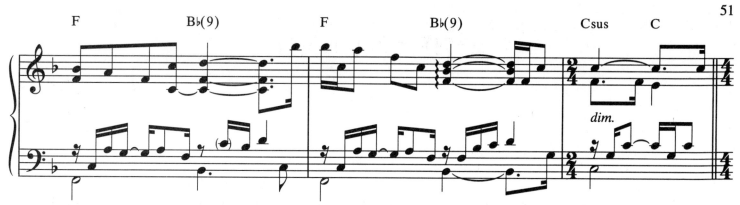

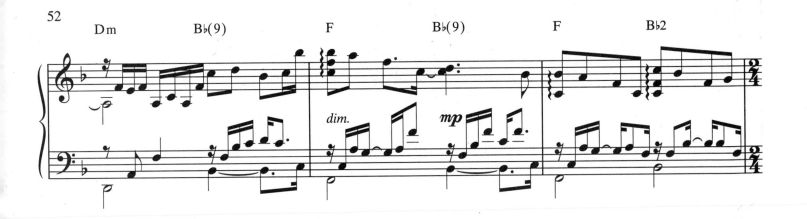

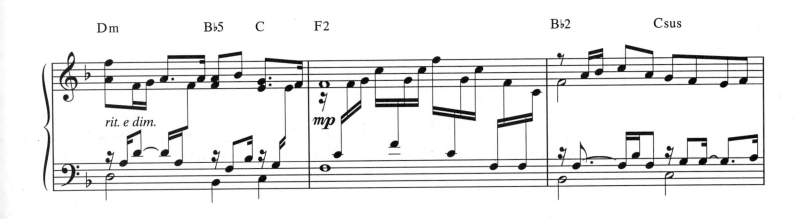